The Return of the Extra

Behind the scenes stories from your favourite TV Detective shows

John R Walker was born in 1972 and was brought up in the West Country.

He always wanted to be a Film Director but ended up spending 20 years in Retail working up from Delicatessen Assistant to Assistant Head of Retail Operations for Safeway and then Head of Internal Corporate Films for WM Morrisons only to leave it all behind to become a full-time TV Extra.

His first TV Extra role was in 1998 for a Doctor Who Spin-off called "Auton 2"

He now lives in Dudley with his family and works at the BBC as a 1st AD on daytime Drama

The Return of the Extra

Behind the scenes stories from your favourite TV Detective shows

John R Walker

With Stephen Hatcher

First Published 2023

This Edition 2023

Copyright John R Walker 2023

ISBN: 9798856369853

Photographs Copyright John R Walker

Cover design Andrew Mark Thompson

"He twinkles in the background-Unrivaled star of the TV extras"

The Guardian

"Who is that with John Walker? The unknown who is on TV most days of the year"

The Daily Telegraph

"The Tesco extra"

The Sun

"TV's most prolific extra- a Tesco worker who's been in 2000 shows and met his fiancée on set"

The Daily Mail

"2000 TV shows make me extra special"

Daily Express

"Who is that with John Walker?"

Daily Star

"Criminal one day, Copper the next- The ultimate Tesco extra"

The Independent

"After 14 years and 2000 appearances on 200 TV shows, actor John Walker is finally playing the lead role in a story"

Daily Mirror

2013 was a strange year. I had released a book called "Extra Time" which told of some of my adventures on the sets of the UK's most loved TV shows but for some reason the press went wild and I'm suddenly voted "Britain's most Prolific TV extra" and I had every UK national newspaper do at least a half page spread each, I had 4 magazine articles in the UK and one in a Portugal magazine, I had top news on Yahoo, MSN and other search engines, I was on the local news as well as 8 Radio Stations around the UK and Ireland and I even turned down "Daybreak" and "BBC Breakfast Show" and all this was because I was trying to get a little local press about my book (The local press gave me full double spread pages) but most of them forgot what I was trying to push and simply made me into this "super" Extra. To the point that to this day, if you Google the word "TV Extra" from the UK, my name is the first to come up.

I'm nothing of the kind. There are guys who've been Extras longer than I have been alive but I have done my fair share and these are just some of the crime and detective shows I've done.

There's so many missing.

Missing notes and days on set I simply can't remember but most of these were written down at the time or when my brain was much more active.

My wife and I used to work on so many crime shows and I'd usually be in the same suit in all of them.

Some stories are taken from my previous book "Extra Time".

If you would like to read more stories from other UK shows then do pick up a copy or grab yourself other "Stories from a TV Extra" pocket books

In the time of writing this I have long given up the extra work and I now earn my pay by being a 1st AD on a BBC Afternoon drama.

I hope you enjoy the book.

All the best

John R. Walker (Aug 23)

For my daughter India

Contents

1. Life on Mars

2. Vincent

3. New Street Law

4. Trial and Retribution

5. Heartbeat

6. Whistle Blowers

7. Lewis

8. Bonekickers

9. Ashes to Ashes

10. Law and Order UK

11. Sherlock

12. The Bill

13. Poirot

14. Hustle

15. 5 Days

16. Marple

17. The Jury

18. Appropriate Adult

19. Midsomer Murders

Life on Mars – Night Clubber

9th June 2005

Up to now I had been very passive in my time as an Extra, accepting whatever work was offered to me, taking pride in never being late and in never saying no. The first show that I actually chased was Life on Mars. The show first caught my attention when I read about it in a magazine. It sounded a little bit science fiction, being about a man from 2006 who gets sent back in time to 1973.

I went to see my booker in Manchester and asked if I could get on it and it proved to be no problem at all. The one great advantage about being in anything that's not set in contemporary times is that we get to dress up, so we don't have to take loads of clothes with us.

I arrived at the location and parked up next to an old brown Cortina, which it turned out, would become famous as Gene Hunt's car. Of course I had no idea at the time that this car would become as important a character as the actors.

We were sent to costume and there on the rack I found a fabulous set of 1970s clothes with my name on.

It wasn't much of a scene, as all we were doing was waiting to get into a club.

It was a wide shot so we didn't really get a close up.

The scene involved a group of 70s party goers waiting to go into a club and queuing outside.

When the scene was set up, everyone was split into boys and girls but unfortunately for me, my screen girlfriend got sent to be a passenger in a passing car so I thought I had to queue on my own but it turned out there was another chap on his own so we became a couple.

It wasn't particularly exciting but I was just glad to get on the show.

Life on Mars – Pub Local
19th/ 20th June 2005

I was lucky enough to be invited back to Life on Mars for a couple of days, to play one of the drinkers in a pub called "The Trafford Arms"

Some of the guys had wigs put on them. I was hoping to get one too as I had a very un-70s style short hair cut.

All the usual crowd were there, about forty of us, who I'd see on most of the jobs that I'd done, so it was great to catch up.

Although we were allocated clothes we could choose what shoes to wear, so when I saw this pink pair with pink ribbons for laces I simply had to have them.

One of the things I found funny about getting onto the 1970s set with our 70s clothes was the fact that we all had our mobile phones stuffed in our pockets!

I spoke to one of the crew who'd seen a finished version of the first episode, as I had said that I was looking forward to the show. He told me that the first episode looked amazing but corrected me when I called it science fiction. To this day I would still call it sci-fi. After all, it's about a man who has travelled in time!!

The pub was a real pub that had been closed down at some point and the production had made it look open and of course period.

It was great to see the action and Philip Glennister was amazing. He had to jump over the bar and he did it so many times.

<u>Vincent</u>

5th March 2006

"Vincent" was an ITV drama that starred Ray Winstone, on which we did a lot of days over a long period. I just remember getting to the location with my friend (back in the days when it used to be the same people on every job), who had just worked a night shift as a taxi driver in Halifax before coming straight to this shoot.

When the extras are kept busy, you can get away with being tired and catch up on sleep that night, but sometimes (most of the time) we're just left waiting all day, doing next to nothing until wrap (which is usually two minutes before overtime).

Well on this occasion we were left in the same seats in a nice warm location all day and not used. My friend just slept the whole day away and got paid for the privilege.

We had zero idea what this show was actually about as we didn't actually do anything worth talking about. Just walking up and down stairs.

<u>New Street Law</u>

Lawyer -7th June 2006

Our Manchester agency had a new booking agent called Charlie whom I loved. He'd come from Red Productions and I hope he's still in the industry somewhere today. What makes a great booking agent is knowing what you look like, what your character is like and how well you can deal with lines if need be and of course how reliable you are. Charlie was brilliant.

On this particular day Charlie had booked us to do "New Street Law". Our agency had the monopoly on this show, which I guess was something to do with Charlie, as it was made by Red Productions.

This was a show about lawyers, (the clue is in the title), and we were asked to bring suits and smart casual wear. My favourite! No scruffy clothes for me today.

There were about thirty of us booked, all from our agency and we took it in turns to go to costume to check what we had with us.

The rumour was going around that lots of people had not brought suits with them and were being sent home.

This turned out to be true. There must have been twenty people who turned up without suits. Now, Extras are not important as far as crew are concernedbut when lots of Extras make a mistake like this, it can cost a production a lot of money as the shoot cannot go ahead as planned.

The 2nd AD was on the phone to the agency in minutes and a call went out to all other Manchester-based extras agencies with the message that all extras had to be suited and ready on set as soon as humanly possible.

I guess the other agencies couldn't believe their luck as this was their chance to slip into this production, which still had a good few months shooting to go, (although the season was actually cut back in the end and then ultimately cancelled.)

Charlie called me up "John, who didn't bring their suits with them today from our agency?" Oh my lord he wanted me to snitch on the other Extras. I didn't have many friends as it was, without blabbing their names out.

"Just check to see who got signed out at eight thirty and who didn't. Those of us who are still here are the ones who brought all the correct costume."

I know Charlie came down to see the production office in person to apologise but I have no idea of the outcome, as I never did that show again. This was a pity as it was a nice show to do. I always judge whether an actor is a nice person or not by their attitude to us.

If they at least acknowledge that we exist, then they're OK by me. Just a nod will do.

John Hannah, the star of New Street Law, was fantastic and spoke to everyone. This pleased me, as I had liked him in the Mummy movies. I hate it when someone whom I have admired turns out to be less than friendly and doesn't even give you eye contact.

The day was spent walking around a big building with a camera on a jib, going up the stairs. I know it doesn't sound too exciting but a lot of these jobs are like this

<u>Trial and Retribution</u> – <u>Public Gallery</u>

Tuesday 31st August / Friday 1st September 2006

I think this was the first time that I worked at Kingston-upon-Thames Courthouse. This has to be one of the most used locations on British television, not just for the court interiors, the exterior makes a good Buckingham Palace too.

This was another case of a not particularly exciting scene or memorable experience. It was however, the day when I was sitting on the bus, somewhere in the middle, with what appeared to be a group of new extras behind me, and a bunch of old hands at the front. The guys at the back were really excited about doing some TV work but the ones at the front wanted nothing to do with them, being as they were, seasoned Extras.

This was the day I learnt a new word. That word is S.A. (Supporting Artiste)

The trouble with being an Extra is that all you need to be able to do is breath and walk. Scrub that, you don't even need to be able to walk. As long as you are alive then you're already as well qualified as you'll ever need to be, to be an Extra!

Just turn up to work and do as you're told. It really is that simple. Unfortunately some people have a problem with the fact that no experience is needed, you need know nothing about film making and you're only there as a breathing prop.

You're not actually involved in the making of the production; you are part of the finished picture, the movement in the background. The job is so demeaning that out-of-work actors are advised to get a job in a fast food retail chain rather than be an Extra.

I'm not slagging the job off, as I absolutely love it. It's brilliant, but it does turn your brain to jelly and can play havoc with your self-worth.

Some Extras having developed a problem with this over time, want to feel important. So they have invented a special term that only extras know - Supporting Artiste.

I've been on set before and seen Extras rip down the sign on the bus that says "Extras Holding Bus", as they're so insulted at being referred to as 'Extras'. The fact that only Extras call themselves S.A.s is beside the point. No one outside the world of the extra knows what an S.A. is!

It's all kind of weird, but unfortunately as I have said many times before, this is the only job in the world that you never move up in.

It doesn't matter if you're an Extra for one job or for forty years, you'll still be just an Extra.

I was still living in Derbyshire at this time and didn't do much London work. The guys at the front of the bus had pretty much ignored me most of the day, assuming, I imagine, that I was a newbie. I started chatting to them and they seemed to be quite impressed that I'd had so many speaking roles. I guessed that they were not as easy to get down South as they were in the North? I had no idea but anyway, this seemed to impress them enough for them to invite me to the front of the bus.

When one of them asked me if I did anything besides "S.A." work I replied that I headed up the internal corporate film department for Morrisons with over 150,000 people withIn the firm. "I'm based at home in

Derbyshire but have an area in the Bradford Head Office."

This piqued their curiosity and one of them asked me why I did "S.A. work". I replied, "Because I enjoy it, it's a bit of fun"

Not the response I expected when they went mad at me. "Fun? This isn't fun. This is people's livelihoods and you're taking work away from people who need it!"

"This isn't work" I objected," no one could possibly do this for a living"! How wrong I turned out to be but that story is for later on.

The other thing I really remember about one of these days is being outside the building looking at the Second World War bullet holes in the wall and having a cigarette when the set medical officer came up to me.

I said Hello but he suddenly laid into me about smoking. If I had seen the things he'd seen, then I wouldn't do it. If I ever got ill from smoking then there would be no way in hell that he would lift a finger to look after me.

He just went mad at me and went on and on. It wasn't like I was even close to him so he'd come over the car park just to say these things to me.

<u>Heartbeat - Give Peace a Chance - Slimy Reporter</u>

Tuesday 12th September 2006

I got a call to say that I had been picked for a speaking role in Heartbeat. Everyone makes fun of my attempts at accents, so I didn't even try to do a Northern one, They sent me the script in the mail which is unusual for an Extra.

My bit was so tiny and unimportant. "Just right for the local rag", I had to say in a slimy reporter kind of way. By now I was beginning to notice that the only speaking roles I ever got had the words 'slimy' or 'mean' in the character description, but anyway, they're usually the fun things to play. I have no problem being funny-looking with a large forehead and slitty little eyes if that's what gets me featured parts.

This was one of those sets where every member of the crew was really fantastic and didn't talk to us like shit. I went to location in a nice car while the other guys were in a big bus. I never heard the end of them taking the mickey, but the great thing about seeing the same old guys on set is that at some point we all get to have a nice role. It's almost like taking it in turns.

I had no problem back then with what people thought us as Extras, as I had a really nice job in real life, with a nice company car and probably got paid better than most of the people on set. However, it was still really nice when a crew treated you well, like you mattered.

This was one of the very few shows that allowed us to take photos all day, as long as we didn't do it during a take.

My first scene was driving past actor John Duttine (who had starred in the classic BBC sci-fi serial 'The Day of the Triffids') in the rather nice 1960's car that I had been given, and then showing him my press pass. John then just had to look at me and say contemptuously, "That's all we need".

I hadn't got much else to do, so I sat there in the sun all day, watching the filming with one of the guys who was playing a photographer. This was one of the few shows that let passers-by stop and watch and meet the actors and even have some tea and biscuits. They were just such a lovely crew.

Finally my big scene arrived. Remember what I have said about speaking Extras? Even these are unimportant. That's why they left me last, right to the end of the day, by which time the light was fading fast. I had learnt my one line and had practiced it for the last twenty-four hours. I had to be word perfect and I wasn't going to mess this up.

The director then said to me and the non-speaking photographer "You guys can say whatever you want just so long as it fits in the scene!"

What?

Why go to all the effort of writing a script and sending it to me, only for my line to be so unimportant that I can say anything I liked? I wasn't having this and I said to the director "No, my line is, 'This'll look right on the front of the local rag, (pause) hey?'"

I shouldn't really have said it but he wasn't in the mood to argue as light was going fast. So the photographer and I walked to the car and I leant over the window to say my line. "This'll look right on the front of the local rag" (pause). Before I could get out my really well practiced "Hey?"

with a nice snarl at the edge of my lip, the photographer extra took his opportunity to throw some lines in "All-right mate, look up!" What? When did he suddenly get lines?

I guess I would have done the same to be fair

It was a one take wonder and we were wrapped.

I saw the episode on TV and to show how unimportant extras really are, they used different extras to play our parts in a later scene, plus they took my line and placed it over a different shot of me, even though my lips weren't moving. At least I wasn't dubbed.

<u>The Whistleblowers – Lawyer</u>

Sunday 18th March 2007

I only wanted to mention this job because it was another one on which they held me back all day, with the promise that I was going to be heavily featured! It was in London at the Kingston- upon-Thames Court House.

The show starred Richard Coyle and the beautiful Torchwood actress Indira Varma. It turned out to be a brilliant show.

I'd not had the chance to see Indira on the Torchwood set so I was very happy to get this small "walk-on".

There were three actors plus me in the scene, two of us on each side of the court with the public sitting behind us. Unfortunately the actor playing the defence lawyer and myself were on the opposite side to

Indira, but nonetheless I was quite excited by the role.

The defence lawyer and I had to be given a message about something, which we had to look at and then do some pretend talking.

Sometimes we extras forget our place and but the truth is when a featured role is given to an Extra it's because it's not big enough to give to a real actor and it would be wrong to get an actor in for something that could quite easily be cut.

When the show was broadcast, I enjoyed every episode, which is quite unusual for me when it comes to TV that's not of a science fiction or cult nature.

When it came to my episode near the end of the series, they had somehow cut me right out, to the point that the cameraman had never even framed me in shot. After so much attention to detail, with my suit and make-up and facial expressions, I wasn't even in the show.

It's a real shame the show was not commissioned for a second series as it was a great show but being cut or maybe never actually being framed in the shots in the first place area gentle reminder that you can never assume that you're going to be in a show, no matter how big your role is, until you actually see it on screen.

A lesson I never seemed to learn.

Lewis – Reporter

Tuesday 28th August 2007

Lewis is one of those shows that I do quite often, but I never take any notice of which episodes I have done as I have never watched the show.

On this particular day I had a line to say. It was just typical that they would give me lines in a show that I never watch. "Inspector Lewis, can you tell me how many officers you have on the scene?",

I had just come off Doctor Who and was desperate to get a line on that one day.

I remember another day I had done on this show, it was really wet, in fact it was pouring down. We were filming inside a museum, or at least in somewhere that was set up to look like a museum.

As I sat there, I saw a very wet young lady walk in at the back of the hall with a hood over her face and a KFC in her hand. I said to the guy next to me, "Look, there's Billy Piper." He wouldn't believe me. "Why would Billy Piper be here? She's not in this show and she wouldn't look like that."

I pointed out whom she was dating, (they're now married). She could afford to look very wet because she was not in the show. As she kissed Laurence Fox and turned to go, the guy next to me finally believed me!

We then got up to do the scene. At the time I had a full time job, as I have mentioned before with a company mobile phone.(remember this was 2007) I didn't want to change my number so I always carried both telephones on me. On set we are told to have our telephones turned off at all times, which seemed silly to me for two reasons.

1. How do I know if someone is calling me if my mobile is off?

2. How come the crew are allowed to keep theirs on? How can you tell me that Extras' phones affect the boom mic, when other people's don't?

So, I had mine on silent.

We were all facing one of the actors who was giving us a speech, when the "cut" was called. Apparently there was phone interference.

The AD shouted at all the Extras, saying that we shouldn't have our phones turned on while on set nor in fact have them with us at all!

He made such a point of it that we all took our phones out of our pockets and made sure they were switched off. "Not on silent – off!"

Of course I just checked that both of mine were on silent!

The scene started again and once again it was cut early, as the sound guy said that there was definitely a mobile phone switched on in the building. This time the crew had to turn theirs off too. I took the hint and turned my private phone off, leaving my work one turned on just in case someone wanted to get hold of me!

The scene started again and once again they cut it due to interference.

This time the AD was so mad, he came right up to the Extras, stood right in front of us and said we'd not turned our phones off and we were wasting their time.

Lunch would be delayed because of it. I felt my pocket vibrating! Someone was trying to get hold of me. I couldn't believe no one else could hear the vibrating but it was too late to turn it off now. Imagine getting the phone out after such a shouting at and turning it off! I'd have been thrown off set. It was best to say nothing and hope they wouldn't notice.

Before you know it, we were being told to take our phones out of our pockets and hold them up. We had to show that our phones were switched off. I took my private phone out and left the other one where it was, wondering who had phoned and wanting to check it.

The 3rd AD reported to the 1st AD that it was none of the Extras and they finally decided that the interference must have been coming from outside the building and that the Extras were innocent after all. They apologised.

But yes, it was me.

<u>Lewis – Passer-by</u>

Monday 11th August 2008,

I was on a show recently where the word 'passer-by' had clearly been decided to be demeaning, so I was called a 'London Onlooker'. It was the whole SA thing all over again!

I was in Oxford and walking to the Lewis production office to sign in when I heard, "Oi, John" from behind me. I turned around and who should be coming out of his trailer but Bryan Dick! I couldn't believe the coincidence as I had only seen him 2 days ago up in Manchester.

I had a chance to tell him that I couldn't believe that I had not realised he was Adam in Torchwood having had spent 2 days with him and even talking to him about the show!

This was one of those days when the Extras were just told to walk up and down the streets close by the main actors, so that the real passers-by could be used too, but a little further away so that it wouldn't be noticed if they stared at the camera!

The Lewis teams are always happy to let the locals cameo in the show and Kevin Whatley speaks to us so we like him!

<u>Lewis- SOCO</u>

Wednesday 7th September 2008,

This was a lunchtime call near Oxford and the crew were off filming when I arrived, so I had to sit and wait most of the afternoon. I had been told to wear a suit but when the costume department saw us, they gave us a big white condom outfit to put on over our regular clothes.

I didn't really know what a SOCO was as this was my first time playing one. (It's actually a Scene of Crime Officer) I felt very silly in the costume. Then I went on to play one most weeks on Midsomer Murders and have also done so on lots of other shows so don't think anything more of it. Remember you have to lose any self-respect in this job.

We got into costume but had to wait until the final scene of the day. It was funny how much effort costume spent on our ties under the outfit, to be filmed in wide shot, in the dark in a maze. I met an Extra called Paul who was really nice and down to earth. I think Paul and I had more fun taking photos of each other in the outfits than anything as we really didn't do much else that day.

We had to wait until the evening so we had a long afternoon just sitting around and eating (as we like to do) before finally when it was dark enough, we were called to set and. We bent over a fake body and that was it. Shot done and we could go home!

<u>Bonekickers - 18th Century British Soldier</u>

Wednesday 13th February 2008

This was a night shoot in Bristol and it was a seriously cold night. We had to get there quite early in the afternoon, as there were quite a few of us, all dressed up and all bewigged. We had been for a fitting a few days before so that everyone was ready, but it still took a while. We couldn't get breakfast until we had been to costume and make-up.

TV has strange working hours, so we are never surprised to be eating breakfast at any time of the day.

A new girl was doing my hair, so things took a little longer and I was becoming quite upset seeing all the others coming in and going out to eat while I was still sitting there, having my hair very slowly curled.

In the end another hairdresser came along and finished the job for her and I just managed to get my breakfast before we had to go on the minibus to the location.

The scene was set during the American War of Independence and involved lots of American soldiers, a number of black slaves and just a few of us British soldiers.

I would have liked to have put on my long johns but the costume I was wearing had short legs, so I wouldn't have been able to get away with it. On the whole I considered myself lucky however, because the poor black guys had to have bare legs and nothing on their feet. It was starting to ice up outside!

After we dropped our bags off in the green room we were sent outside to have musket training – another of the many weapons that I have had to learn to use since doing this job.

The director James Strong came over to see us. I had met him on Doctor Who when his Christmas episode, Voyage of the Damned, which had featured Kylie Minogue, had broken all records for viewing figures.

As a Doctor Who fan, I had to say Hi and congratulate him on the Christmas special. I love his work and it was a great pleasure to be on his set again. Call me what you will and I'm sorry if I'm now coming over as one of those boring, ass-kissing Extras, but I'm always going to be keen to express my appreciation when I'm on something science fiction related! (Gosh I'm a sad individual)

After gun training we were sent to set to get some shots in before it got dark. We British soldiers were being ambushed. One guy had to have a fight with a stunt man so he got some training prior to the take.

I was the first to be killed, shot in the back and falling forwards as if the bullet had passed right through me. The floor was a stony path, which hurt like mad; but to be fair, it's not often we get so much action, so no one minded a few cuts and scratches.

After I was shot and the other three chaps were also dead, one of the 'Americans' was to stab me in the gut to finish me off. I'd always wanted to do the "being finished off" bit where lifting my legs and arms in one final breath of life. I'm proud to say that the actor finishing me off had been the lead in the London theatre run of the Lion King! If you're going to be killed, be killed by someone cool! The bad guys then had to rob our corpses of our guns.

Unfortunately, my gun had become caught in my wig. He kept pulling and pulling at it and I was trying to be dead while at the same time not letting him move the gun. It would have taken all night to get that bloody hair back on.

Luckily they called cut and the hair stayed. My killer had noticed the problem, and for his part, was not trying too hard to get the gun.

The final shot before it got dark was to be a close-up of me, being shot. I was going to be squibbed (a squib is an electronic gun shot on either a person or object).

It was a race against time. At one point I had seven people around me. My trousers were around my knees and my jacket was open. I was having wires put down my trousers and out the bottom, that would be attached to the Visual Effects box; the costume people were cutting a hole in my jacket for the rip to open and attaching a blood filed rubber with an explosive to the inside; meanwhile make-up were doing my hair and powdering my face. This was all happening at the same time!

I liked the attention to be honest. Who wouldn't?

The scene was easy. An 'American soldier' would fire his musket; the camera would pull focus from him to me and one step, two step, bang! I would look surprised and fall out of frame!

There could only be one take at this as the light was fading fast. There wasn't even time for a rehearsal.

You can feel a squib going off. It's no more than like just being lightly tapped, so I knew that it had gone off early. "Action! - Bang, One step" and the squib went off. Realising what had happened, I fell.

James Strong went mad! What was that? It was supposed to happen on the second step. Luckily he didn't seem to be shouting at me, so I figured I had done what I was supposed to, however the camera hadn't pulled focus in time and the shot had been lost.

James shouted to everyone to set me up again so suddenly I had about seven people all over me again and I just stood there with my trousers around my ankles while the costume was cleaned and sewn up; SFX put a new squib on me and wired it; and make-up cleaned me up after my face first fall onto the floor. (Stunts had given me knee pads this time).

They all worked as fast as they could but the light was nigh on gone and the camera crew couldn't hold out much longer.

Just as I was ready for the retake, James called "Lunch!" We had run out of light!

Special Effects came back over to take the new squib out. "He's not happy with you" I was told.

"Me?" I replied in shock. "This is all my fault?"

"Yes, you fell at the wrong time and they missed the shot"

I was devastated. When any crew member says something like to that to one of us, then it must be true!

I got my lunch and went onto the dining bus. There was my directing hero sitting at a table with the director of photography, looking moody as hell.

I went up to him and said "I'm so sorry about that".

He just looked at me and said unconvincingly "It's okay".

I was so upset. How could I have let down a brilliant Doctor Who director? This isn't a cool job after all, when things like that can happen. Don't work with your idols!

After lunch The Americans were being used and we Brits had nothing to do but wait in the warm, which was rather nice, as it had got seriously cold now that it was dark.

Later, we were called so that we could be shot again, although we were supposed to be different soldiers than earlier, and this was more of a silhouette shot.

I asked the 1st AD if we were being squibbed up for this one and he said no, as we were being shot in the back and there wasn't time.

I told him how glad I was, after I had messed the earlier one up.

"Messed up?" he said "You didn't mess it up".

I told him that Special effects had told me I had.

"Are you kidding? They messed it up by setting off the squib too early".

It was just as I had thought. I hadn't let James Strong down at all! All was better in the world and I loved this job again.

Well, we all tried really hard to get the scene complete first time as it was a tad chilly and the crew were running behind, so we were given numbers one to four. I was to go down on the first shot, on the second shot it was the next guy's turn and so on.

We did as we were told and played dead lying in the frozen grass for ages. It was tough holding my breath after walking and falling down. Usually when I'm dead, I start off dead.

We managed it and were sent back again to warm up until we were needed again.

It was getting late before I was finally called back out for a fight scene with explosions and everything, but I had to remain close to camera, dead lying over metal cannon, for the whole sequence.

I was standing there waiting to go outside onto set and starting to shake with the cold. My teeth were rattling. All of a sudden I felt someone put their hand down my backside, I turned and it was the costume lady, putting a warmer thing down the base of my spine to warm me up.

It didn't help much, but soon afterwards I was put into place. The cannon was so unbelievably cold that I was surprised that my face didn't freeze to it.

I lay there and although I knew that there was going to be an explosion and when it was going to go off, I still found myself jumping every time.

That wasn't why I was sent back in though. I was so cold that my whole body was shaking and there was nothing I could do to stop it. Not ideal when you're supposed to be dead!

So, I was sent indoors, to be replaced by Kristian. He was pleased! (Sorry Kristian to leave you out in the cold sir!).

That was about it for Bonekickers, which was one of the few shows that I have been in that I watched on TV. It was a show that was hated by the critics and became known as one of those shows that was so bad it became funny, but I actually really liked it. Every episode started well and was great until about three quarters of the way through; but then went off into some stupid climax. For me, being a West Country guy, it was great to see my home town on Television.

Ashes to Ashes: Traitor – Dawid Czarnecki

Tuesday 13th January 2009

I had finally got Ashes to Ashes. I was dying to do this show as I had loved Life on Mars so much. I was booked as a Polish worker called Dawid Czarnecki. To do Ashes and to play a named character was brilliant.

The plan was for me to do a scene as living Dawid at a later date, but today I had been booked as his dead body, covered in cement freshly dug out of a cement pit!

I got to set and signed in. Then I was taken to costume. I hate it when I'm not forewarned about something, so it came as a shock when all they gave me was one small pair of flesh coloured pants, plus a dressing gown to put on after filming.

Then I was sent to make-up. Typical! They were all girls. Not a bad thing when they're putting your face on, but I had to lose the gown and stand there in my flesh coloured pants while they painted my body top to bottom with something that looked like cement. I also had to have chain marks put on my ankle and Polish writing on my arm.

Whilst standing there looking naked and dirty with two ladies at my feet, the door suddenly opened and in walked Keeley Hawes.

She didn't even act surprised by the naked looking figure in front of her, she simply held out a hand and introduced herself.

The set was another walk down the road from the base but most people were already there by the time I was called, so I had to make that walk on my own, bare footed and looking like

I'd just got out of bed, in my dressing gown, but with a grey head and face!

At the set door, I was met by the runner and a chap named Charlie Roe who played the pathologist. He was shown to his dressing room while I was taken to the kitchen to wait. It was nice to finally meet the other Extras who work as DCIs on the show. I have since become very good friend with two of them, Jack and Adrian.

I had to wait a while and then was taken into another make-up room for touch-ups. The other main actors were there, and they were very nice to me.

Then I was taken onto set and put onto the slab. The slab is simply a very cold metal bed that you are laid out on when you are dead. I had a blanket under part of my back, as it was very cold but I wouldn't take long to warm up again. So, I lay there with a towel over my flesh coloured pants and then a cloth placed over my entire body.

The pathologist lent over to talk to me, smiled and asked, "How come you get a name? I'm just 'Pathologist' and I've got fucking lines!"

I replied "That's why you get a dressing room and I get shoved into the kitchen!"

The first AD introduced himself and then introduced Keeley Hawes and Philip Glenister. I said that Keeley and I had met already, but then I tried to say something nice to Philip. I hadn't been watching his show "Demons" that was currently on TV, but I'd heard that it had had a slating, so I said "Hello Philip, I'm really enjoying "Demons" right now.

Instead of the expected "Thank you," Philip looked at me and said "Well you're the only fucking one."

I decided not to mention it again, and realised that I'd still not learnt the lesson. Do not mention other shows to actors!"

In the scene, Philip and Keeley's characters had to talk about my body and the marks and writing on my arm. I had to take a breath in the middle of it as it was nearly two minutes long. Holding your breath on TV is far tougher than in real life as you are under real pressure not to mess up the take.

It was a fun scene and once again I was nearly naked on one of my favourite shows, (Doctor Who, Torchwood, The Sarah-Jane Adventures and now Ashes to Ashes)

With the scene complete the crew and actors said goodbye but I had to wait as the art department wanted to take photos, to be used later in the episode. I found it weird watching the episode with the characters handing out my photos to people asking if they knew who I was.

When the art department had finished and I was cleared to go, I asked if I could look around the studio as I was a fan of the show. They were happy for me to have a wander. I wish I had been clean enough to have had my photo taken on the police station set, which was bigger in real life than I had expected.

I had to walk back to base on my own again and I spoke to the 2nd AD about getting cleaned up prior to going home. He found me a spare room with a shower and it was nice to finally get that stuff off me. I'd left marks everywhere I had been and I'd not been able to go to the toilet!

I was booked to come back on the Friday and figured that this would be when I would actually die.

<u>Ashes to Ashes - Dawid Czarnecki</u>

Friday 16h January 2009

I was really looking forward to coming back to die. I had a late call time but, as always, got there early.

When I signed in and was told to wait, I decided to look at the really nice Bentley that was parked at the base. I guessed it was for the actors.

I was asked to go to costume but they only had a shirt and jumper for me. Nothing for the waist down. I asked why and it turned out that I was only having my photograph taken for a passport that was being used in the show.

I was disappointed but I guessed that meant that I would get another day on the show. I went to make-up and then waited to go to set. The 2nd AD came and told me to get into the car. "The Bentley?"

"Yes, It'll take you to set" he said.

I didn't understand why I was being driven to set this time when I looked perfectly normal, but when I was covered in cement I had to walk!

I got in the car. Wow! It had leather seats and everything, but the drive was over all too quickly and I arrived on set, where I was greeted by the runner and then sent up to the art department. I was asked to stand by the wall for a few photos and that was it. I was done!

It had to be the quickest time on set ever. The car took me back to base where I changed and went to see the 2nd AD to sign out. I asked if I was due back to do the death scene, but it seemed that that scene had been cut.

<u>Law and Order UK – Solicitor</u>
Wednesday 21st January 2009

This was a brand new show which featured both Freema Agyeman (Doctor Who) and Jamie Bamber (Battlestar Galactica). I was looking forward to it.

I wasn't in a scene with Freema but when we bumped into each other she said "Hi" and we briefly talked about her small role in Survivors.

I was in a scene with Jamie Bamber, Bradley Walsh and another actor in the interview room. All I had to do was take notes for the other actor as if I was his solicitor, but during the day I got a call from a friend to ask if I had seen the previous night's episode of Battlestar Galactica? I said I hadn't, and would have to wait for the DVD release.

He told me that they had given away who the final Cylon was (a major plot reveal). This was a bad thing as I knew everyone would be talking about it and I would find out before I actually got to see the show.

So I sat down with the actors for the scene and I told Jamie what had happened. As I would soon find out who the final Cylon was without wanting to, would he mind being the one to ruin it for me, as being spoilt by the show's main actor would be a pretty cool way to be spoilt, if it had to happen.

Jamie reassured me that the previous night's episode had been a red herring and advised me to sit tight and not read anything until I got to watch the show.

It was a fun day as all I had to do was sit and write with a serious face on.

Bradley Walsh was a joy. He was so funny and the scene was split for lunch (Meaning exactly as it sounds that we shot some before lunch and some after)

After lunch we went to go back to the scene and Bradley had had a lunchtime sleep.

We rehearsed the scene and Bradley just made all his lines up. They didn't match at all. Then he started laughing and said they shouldn't split scenes because he'd had a sleep and forgotten all his lines.

Everyone was amused. It didn't take long for him get them back in his head.

Law and Order UK- Series 4 – CPS

Monday 14th January 2013

After such a long time without doing Extra work I happened to have a week off my real job so I called up the agencies and asked if there was any work going.

My London agency were first to get back to me and offered me a few jobs. The first of which was this.

There was a severe weather warning and there was a lot of snow on the ground for a 07.15 call time.

I went with my partner and we got to Longcross studios, parked up at the carpark on the outskirts of the studio but the security guard said we were welcome to park up by the set.

So we got back into the car and went through the gate to where the Law and Order studio is.

There was a runner standing out in the cold pointing the way for Law and Order cars to park. We parked up and as soon as we got out of the car he said "I'm sorry but SAs aren't supposed to park up here. You're to park outside the studio and walk up.

Suddenly I'm reminded straight away what I'd been missing! I had only been remembering the fun stuff and had forgotten how you're made to feel when you're on set.

So we drove off and grabbed our gear and walked back to set.

We sighed in and it turned out there were only 4 of us in today. I was jolly pleased to see the amazing Amanda Mealing is in this show and so was former Doctor Who Peter Davison.

The studio was so cold but there were 4 seats and a heater waiting for us so it wasn't all bad.

Peter said Good morning to us when he came onto set. That was pretty cool.

Over the course of the whole day I only made it onto set once. This was sitting in a backroom playing with paperwork. The really weird thing was that the paperwork I was playing with was old Tesco files from the 1980s! How random considering that's where I work now since giving Extra work up in 2012.

My partner went back onto set without me and overheard Peter Davison talking to the other actor. She came back and said she's got some gossip. I'm always all ears for juicy on set gossip and usually I don't repeat it but by the time you're reading this you'll know if it was true!

The other actor asked Peter if he was having anything to do with Doctor Who's 50th Anniversary. Peter replied that he'd had a meeting with Steve Moffatt last week.

Wow...Is he coming into the show for the 50th anniversary special episode?

I got changed so many times today but as I said I only made it to set once.

I got to read a lot of my book today which was nice but the truth is , today reminded me that I'm not really missing doing this job.

I think I needed that reminder and it's mostly how you're made to feel but also I'm at a point I need something more to get my teeth into.

Sherlock (TV Pilot) – Policeman
Wednesday 28th January 2009

I got a call asking if I was available to do Sherlock in Cardiff. I assumed that it was the Guy Richie film and that it must have now relocated to Wales.

I agreed to the job but then found out that it was a night shoot. This was an issue as I had to be on the other side of London by 07.00 the next morning for another show.

I thought nothing more about the job but was a little baffled when I turned up and thought it was rather a small base for a Hollywood movie. (Plus they were sharing it with Doctor Who)

It was only when I went to costume and was given my outfit that I realised that it wasn't the Guy Ritchie movie at all, but a pilot for a modern day set TV show.

Tonight's scene was the very end of the episode and was a single shot of a five minute scene, so it took hours to choreograph the whole thing.

Before we got onto set with our police outfits on, we were spoken to by the AD. They told us it was a criminal offence to pretend to be real police on the streets and so we had to cover our uniforms at all times. We already knew this but I mention it here for a reason.

We rehearsed the scene over and over. I wasn't to join in until half way through.

We were filming on the streets of Cardiff, so real life passers-by were a hazard. At one point four chaps who had come out of the pub were being a little bit naughty and refusing to get out of the way.

The scene had started and the cameras were rolling, while I stood back waiting to enter the scene, with my coat off and in full police uniform.

One of the crew members went up to the guys and asked if they wouldn't mind moving as they were likely to get into shot. They were having none of it, so I was asked if I would go and ask them to move. This was a member of the same crew that had made such a big deal of impersonating a police officer earlier, now getting me to do just that. Anyway, I went up to them and politely asked them just to move around the corner a little. They were a little hesitant at first as they weren't sure if I was a real policeman or not, but as the show was being filmed, clearly without me in it, they seemed to decide that I was for real and gave up and moved along.

I was starting to panic because I was worried about getting to the set of the other show in the morning.

At lunch time I swapped base to say "Hi" to some of the Doctor who crew I knew who were filming "Planet of the Dead" just down the road. The scene involved lots of police, investigating a bus that had gone into a tunnel but not come out. I really wanted to swap shows, I was already in the right uniform after all, but unfortunately it doesn't work like that.

I thought that as we only had one scene, we would be wrapped quite early but it was a tough scene and so many things kept going wrong.

We finally wrapped at 03.45. The other Extras knew that I was desperate to go so they let me get changed first. I ran to the changing room, changed, threw my uniform back to costume, ran to the production office to sign out and jumped into the car.

I had set my sat-nav up earlier and so I turned it on and set off as fast as I could for London. I hadn't got a mile down the road when I realised that the tunnel ahead of me had been blocked for the filming Doctor Who! Normally I would have loved to have stopped and watched the filming, but this time Doctor Who was a source of frustration as I had to take the long way round to get out of Cardiff. It was 178 miles to the next location. I drove as fast as I could and made it out set at 06.50. Just in time for a coffee and to sign in!

<u>Sherlock – City Trader and Baker street pedestrian</u>

Saturday 6th March 2010

The show had shifted from its Cardiff home to London for exterior location shots and interiors that aren't available in Wales so for the first half of the day we were based in a city building near Canary Wharf and it was again nice to catch up with many people I'd not seen since Gulliver's.

My partner was with me and we were all positioned in a seat in this office interior and told that we were city traders so we were to make it look like we were buying and selling shares .

This seemed like lots of fun.

We did this for most the morning as Benedict Cumberbatch came into the office and sneaked around. My girlfriend was asked to do a little action for a cut away. I was so pleased for her as she would get a nice close-up.

I did a few stand ups and looks around but nothing that I thought would get into shot.

Then we were told we had to move to a new location and that we would need to bring our own vehicles if we had them with us.

The next location was a street in North London that was being used a Baker street so we got in the car and put the new address into the Sat - Nav.

We drove to the top of town and found the location. Catering were there dishing out lunch and we had to find somewhere to park. There were several cars driving around in circles just trying to find parking but we finally did and then had lunch.

We were then changed and told the rest of the day were outside shots of 221b Baker street and we were pedestrians.

There weren't that many of us to be fair so we all got used in every scene.

At one point I was standing outside pretty close to Mark Gatiss so decided to do something we're specifically told not to do. I went to say 'Hello'.

"Hello Mark, sorry to bother you but I just wanted to say Hi. I'm a big Doctor Who fan and I've enjoyed your episodes"

That was it. That was all I wanted to say. BUT Mark replied how much he also loved Doctor who and the conversation grew and grew. I'm not sure how long we stood there chatting but it was great and he's so humble. It was brilliant. It's one of the reasons I love this job. We talked so much WHO!

<u>Sherlock – Hiker</u>

Monday 16th May 2011

I got a friend request and a message from someone I didn't know over the weekend. The message said "I'm working with you on Monday and are you coming through Cardiff and can you give me a lift?"

I've never had a good experience giving people lifts and I had no idea who this chap was so I ignored it

This was one of those jobs that was seriously in the middle of nowhere at a farm base that my sat nav had no idea how to get to. It was lucky I was sent a movement order to get me there.

Sat nav's are brilliant but film/TV bases are usually not on the road but in an unnamed back road around the back of places so it's always good to look up where you're going on the internet.

I got to set jolly early and had an hours sleep prior to starting at 07.00. I was booked as a hiker and I made the mistake of taking my shorts with me as a costume option.

They put me in the shorts and they gave me a big coat and some hiking style socks to wear. Nice.

I went to the Extras bus to wait until we were going on set and the chap who'd messaged me came up to me and asked if I'd gotten his note? I said I had but wasn't aware that I knew him so I ignored it (Was that rude of me?)

We went to set which was in fact just a pub up the road In a tiny village. The DOP (Director of Photography) was a guy called Fab who I had got to know from Survivors,Scott & Bailey and DCI Banks so it was nice to see him.(He went on to do the Justice League movie)

Both Benedict Cumberbatch and Martin Freeman were in good spirits and said good morning to us. Then I saw Mark Gatiss. I said Hello and then the strangest thing happened.

He came up to me and said "Congratulations"

I was both dumbfounded and confused. Why has he said this to me, does he think I'm somebody else?

So "Congratulations for what?" I asked

"On the magazine article in woman's own the other week" he replied.

Now, this information was true, my partner had had a two page spread in Woman's own magazine about how we had met on set and about the Extra work we do.

I was so embarrassed. This meant a couple of things.

1- It meant that Mark Gatiss knows who I am since we met on the first Sherlock series and that means he knew who I was when I saw him in London a few months back and got his autograph and a photo with him. How embarrassing.

2- It also meant that he thinks I have a really sad existence as a full time Extra (Unfortunately this part is true which makes it worse)

I told him that it was my partners article and not mine but he pointed out (As he must have a super memory) that I was quoted too.

I was quoted to saying "Being an Extra is the best job in the world"

So I told Mark the actual quote that I gave the magazine when they asked which was "Being an Extra should only be considered a hobby and you've got to be very sad with no career prospects if you do this full time for a living and that I'm trying to get out of it" but I guessed that quote didn't work well for the article and they slightly updated. He said that's what the press do.

I still couldn't believe he'd read it (and why was Mark Gatiss reading woman's own?)

I told him that if it had been my article then it would have gone on about Dr Who and Sherlock. (as you may notice, that's all I go on about and so I see that many reviewers of my last book have mentioned)

And then on the subject of Doctor Who we discussed last week's episode (The Doctors wife) and he said he preferred the first 2 parter this season. That's one of the reasons I love Mr. Gatiss.

He's a successful and very talented actor/writer and producer but when it comes to Doctor Who. He's just a fan like the rest of us and it's just the same as talking to any other fan when you get to talk to him about the show.

The scene was only Sherlock and Watson walking into a pub and saying a couple of lines but for some reason this took the whole day.

We were hikers that walk past as he enters the pub and that's all there was.

At the end of the day I ran to the car and got changed and then ran to costume to return the Coats and socks and then got my Chit signed and ran to the car to avoid having to give people a lift. I got back home at 22.00 only to have to get up again at 03.30 for the next day.

The Bill – Policeman

Wednesday 25th March 2009

On a show like The Bill they have regular police and CID extras, but in between the gaps between the scenes they have something called establishing shots.

These tell the audience where the next scene is taking place, (in the show of course, not necessarily in real life). So that the establishing shots can be slotted into the show at any time in any episode they deliberately don't use any of the police or CID extras that are in the show regularly, as this might cause continuity problems.

This was an establishing shot day, so we spent the whole day outside the police station walking about, backwards and forwards, getting into cars and back out again. It went on for twelve hours and was a tad tiring.

The police station used in the Bill in an actual building in the middle of a trading estate, although all the signs for the station were taken down between shoots. On this occasion however, all the signage was up and the lights on. Inevitably, while we were doing one take, a car pulled up and a girl got out thinking it was a real police station.

Security explained that this was just a TV set and they later told me this happens all the time when they set up the station.

We did loads and loads of episodes worth of shots on this day.

The Bill – Football supporter
11/12/15/16/21 February 2010

We filmed the Bill just down the road from Millwall at Elephant and Castle and I decided to check out the location the night before to find local parking but there simply wasn't any to be found. I spent ages driving up and down roads to see if I could save on time and money so in the end I decided to park back towards Millwall. (It was a road about a mile from the location and some days I used the bus but some days I walked it)

We were doing what was to become one of the last episodes of the show and I was playing one of very many football supporters.

 We were in a scene where we had either won or lost a game and decided to tackle to police on our way home but the police were very understaffed on the day.

There must have been about 300 of us supporters and we spent many hours doing crowd replication so we would stand in place and chant and then they would cut and we would mix up and stand behind where we had been standing and per my previous job in a football stadium.

When it actually came to the confrontation with the police I decided to stay at the front and I had my own flag prop that I had been handed for the shoot.

The location we were using is an old council estate where the local council had relocated many of the occupants so they can knock it down and re build the place. The location gets used a lot (Ashes to Ashes, Harry Brown and even Clint Eastwood used it recently to make his film) but there are a handful of people left in the estate.

On one of the days we were chanting at the police and suddenly this chap starts swearing at us from one of the upper flats.

The Extras found this really funny but we were told by the crew to ignore him. Well the man simply didn't stop. He shouted and shouted and then started to put some music on seriously loud.

It got to a point that they couldn't record any sound and with so many people on set it was starting to cost them money.

The crew decided to pay the man some money (More than we were getting I'm told) to go out shopping for the day.

Whereas up in his flat he looked like a scary scruffy chap, by the time he came down it looked completely different (This has no relevance to the story but something I noted) and when he did come down he started to shout at the Extras from a bridge and the Extras were all cheering him until we were told not to by the crew.

He was telling us we're working for rubbish pay and to stop doing it and go home. It was weird as he obviously knew how much we were earning and we figured he must do this to every film crew just to get some easy money for the day.

After that excitement it was back to the chanting and pretending to chant whilst the actors did their dialogue.

Then the fun began as we had to slowly move forwards toward the police. I spoke to the policeman in front of me and he said he was a stunt man. I asked if he happened to be Derek Lea from Highlander TV show and Torchwood? He was. He'd had some nice acting roles in both of them and I'd spotted him in Doctor Who many times.

It was great to chat to him. We're not allowed photos with actors on set but no one has ever told me not to get a photograph with a stuntman!

The stuntmen were mixed in with us at the front rows as both police and supporters (and sometimes swapping out to be both)

The next scene was the riots. Now riots are organised and done slowly and carefully on film. Always. That is why Stunts are brought in so that we are all kept safe.

The police line was in front of us and all we have to do is shout at them and 'pretend' to push forwards but not actually push as it's just a TV show .

Typically and as always with these things, there were some who decided to disregard all this. There's always a few blighters who get more and more carried away and find it funny to really push the police and to push those of us at the front forwards towards the police. It was getting silly, add to that I have a large wooden stick with a flag on it so it wasn't easy to not knock into people with that.

We did the scenes over and over and the stupid ones were getting worse. It got to a point where I decided not to be at the front any more so I went right to the back.

Now this was really weird. Having been at the forefront of all the action earlier, now I was at the back with the guys who simply didn't do anything. I mean anything. It was like just a jolly day out and no one was taking any notice if they were filming or not. They figured the camera couldn't see them back here so you wouldn't have known when it was action and when it wasn't.

Finally over the course of the days we broke the police lines and went running off in every direction.

On one of the days a few of us were asked to stay behind when most of the others were wrapped (Always wrapped before overtime kicked in) and there was a scene of the aftermath of the riots with just a few of us rioters left behind and being told to go home.

Well I was with my friend and we decided to look like we were falling out with the 2 police Extras as they had come along and we all needed something to do.

It seemed the director liked it and swapped the Extra policemen into 2 of the regular actor policemen. The 2 actors grab us and shout at us and send me packing whilst cuffing my friend.

The shot was only a wide so there we weren't particularly prominent but the interaction with the actors meant we got extra money. Nice to think we got our own 'Walk ons' by making up what we were doing in the first place.

Poirot: The Clocks – Special Agent

Tuesday 23rd June 2009

Hayes, Middlesex. This was a blighter of a studio to find first time. Nonetheless I found it and it turned out to be a very friendly crew indeed. The 3rd AD came into the bus to see me and gave me the sides for the day. (Sides are the parts of the script that are being filmed on that particular day and are usually fixed onto the back of the call sheet). This doesn't happen very often but it's very nice when it does as we know then what the scene is about and how long we will be expected to be on set.

When I looked through the call sheet I saw Tom Burke's name and froze. Tom was the actor whom I loved in the film "I Want Candy" but when I had spoken to him he had hated it and wasn't afraid to tell me his thoughts on the film! I went to costume to get into my 1940s gear. I seem to spend a lot of time in period clothes..

It was a shame that David Suchet wasn't on set that day as I really wanted to see him working as Hercule Poirot.

My role was to walk some suspect or other to the cells... I think.

It was a set that had been made to look like some tunnels where they had filmed in down in Portsmouth. My friend Adrian was there, whom I had gotten to know on Gulliver's Travels. (He had also been one of the regular CID guys on Ashes to Ashes).

On set I bumped into Tom Burke. I said Hello and he returned the greeting. I could see that he recognised me from somewhere and I was terrified that he would realise that I was the one whom he had shouted at in Bristol.

He asked if we'd met before and I told him it was on another period piece in Bristol. Oh, "In Love with Barbara" he said, although it hadn't been called that when we shot it

I said I thought it was called something else but he told me they'd changed the name of the show.

He had no idea that I was the "I Want Candy" fan.

Poirot – Policeman

Monday 12th - Thursday 15th October 2009

I always love doing the Agatha Christie shows so I was very pleased to be offered several days on Poirot. Even better, the episode (called Halloween Party) was written by Mark Gatiss for whom I have a lot of respect, as he is a brilliant actor/writer.

Unfortunately I didn't get to see Mark on the set but as always with these productions, there was an amazing cast, which included Zoë Wannamaker and Julian Rhind-Tutt.

According to the script I was part of a "gaggle" of police.

How many is a gaggle you ask? Well there are in fact only two of us for this entire episode.

My fellow police officer was an old friend of mine called Ian, with whom I had spent a lot of time on Gulliver's Travels, struggling to learn that dance and more recently realised we did Toast of London together.

The location was the garden of a very old house near Windsor, with topiary hedges cut into amazing shapes. Ian and I had to start off hiding in the garden. Then when Poirot (David Suchet) called out we had to run out of the hedges, chase and arrest Julian Rhind-Tutt.

Julian turned out to be a lovely down to earth chap. I think I had seen him on TV as a bad guy so many times, that I didn't expect him to be so nice.

Something that was weird and not what I was used to was being asked to be a little rough with him when we captured and arrested him.

We spent the rest of the week pretty much walking around the gardens and the lakes near the house.

Everybody on this show was fantastic and kind and there was so much respect for David Suchet.

 Ian and I were even given chairs to sit on while we were waiting around but on the opposite side of that, it was a little surprising, considering we were the only 2 Extras on set when we were in the queue for lunch and then the AD came along and said "Come on you guys, you know the rules. Get to the back of the queue".

I know this is the policy but we thought it might be different as there were only two of us.

So we went to the back and waited, while more and more crew kept popping up out of no-where. Just when it seemed we were getting near the front yet more crew would appear and we'd have to wait a bit longer. I am pleased to report that we did manage to eat in the end though.

<u>Poirot – Policeman</u>

Thursday 22nd -Friday 23rd October 2009

Ian and I were back on Poirot for another 2 days, which was the dénouement of the episode. We had each been given sides.

(Yeah, I had to look up the word dénouement too)

I sat at the side of the room looking at the sides and watching what was going on but keeping out of the way until required. We watched a pre-camera blocking and rehearsal.

All the actors were in their respective seats and the 1st AD called action just to see the scene for the first time.

David Suchet started talking. Without reference to any sides he did the entire thirteen page dénouement scene, straight off, word perfect. I had never seen anything like it. It was amazing. Even some of the other actors who were in the room, who had very little to say still had a set of sides in their hand as back-up.

He was such a joy to watch working plus he keeps the Belgian accent on between scenes so when he speaks to you.

All Ian and I had to do was bring the handcuffed Julian Rhind-Tutt into the room, then to stand there with him in front of us. It wasn't much, but it was a real honour to see David Suchet at work.

At the end of the second day all the actors wanted to have their photos taken together, so Ian and I were asked to take it in turns to take the photos and to stand in them in our period police outfits. Of course we wanted to get the pictures on our cameras too, but alas you know the rules on set. No extras can take photos but it's nice to know they're out there somewhere.

<u>Hustle – Diner</u>

Friday 28th August 2009

We were booked as diners on Hustle, which by now was filming in Birmingham, having moved out of London, (although it still pretended to be in London).

Another bonus about this job is that sometimes we get to go to places where we wouldn't normally be welcome. That day we were in a very expensive and I imagine very exclusive diners' club in the centre of Birmingham.

The guest actor in this episode was Daniel Mays, whom at the time I had never heard of, but who has since become famous for his electrifying performances in Ashes to Ashes, Doctor Who, Treasure Island, Mrs Biggs and almost everything else that has been good on television in recent years. He proved to be very friendly, speaking to everybody. He was, however very loud, but I guess that was just the character he was playing.

The waiter in this episode was played by a friend of mine called Adam Fray. He sounded pretty pleased and pleasantly surprised about getting this job.

Adam was really cool and didn't have any of the "us and them" attitudes that actors sometimes have. Being new to TV he'd not yet learnt how low we Extras are on the ladder.

I mention Adam because we worked together on a low budget film previously called "Deadtime" but I was on the other side of the camera for that one.

I was sitting with my real life partner and two Extras who had never done it before. Now, the last thing an Extra should ever do is to give advice to other Extras, as we're all at the bottom of the pile together, but on this occasion, I broke that rule.

Don't hate me, who am I to give advice to anyone? But these two ladies, along with the rest of us, had been told to mime. Surely, miming is not a difficult concept to grasp, but you wouldn't believe how many people seem to feel that when they mime, they have to over-compensate for the lack of sound coming out of their mouths.

People suddenly start waving their arms around and nodding their heads wildly.

Many even confuse miming with whispering. I don't think they understand just how much sound the microphone picks up. You can whisper across the room and it will be picked up by the sound guys. This was very much one of those bad miming occasions.

Background sometimes fall into four categories: Firstly there are the whisperers, who come in very close to each other, so as to hear what the other person is saying. This looks very silly as generally people don't get that close whilst chatting.

Then there are the pointers, the over compensating mimers, who have to exaggerate every single movement of their bodies while pretending to talk non-stop with big wide open mouths. Oh, and they have to point!

The Zombies are those extras who are never quite comfortable when a camera is pointed in their direction. They just can't relax. They can be spotted by their strange zombie walk, with eyes forward, arms straight down at their sides, almost as if they are being pulled along on a trolley!

Finally there are the rhubarbs, normal, relaxed, comfortable Extras who just mime and respond to other people's mimes, even though neither has any idea what the other is talking about. They move as little and as often as necessary to keep the scene alive but at the same time they don't distract the audience from the main performance.

Well, on his occasion we had two pointers on our table! They were talking non-stop, making it look like they were talking over each other and pointing at everything they could see!

My partner and I just read the menu and ignored them out of shame!

I tried to say nothing but finally had to point this out politely to them and suggested that it might be an idea if they were to look at each other, so one wasn't talking over the other. Does this make me a bad person?

They were new and were very polite about it.

Hustle – All night Gambler
Thursday 25th August 2011

I felt really ill on this day and luckily my partner was working with me as there was no way I could drive and I refused to go sick.

We were good friends with the 3rd AD on this as he'd been our 3rd on Scott and Bailey.

We were playing casino goers but had been informed that last year when Hustle had filmed here, an Extra had decided to steal some of the chips and maybe come back to cash them in another day when the casino was open. More fool him as the casino staff caught him on camera and the crew made every effort to let him return them without saying they knew who it was.

He finally left them in the Toilets and made out he'd seen them there and that somebody else must have left them but was not aware all of his actions were being recorded on CCTV. Anyhow, we were told this story by an embarrassed crew member who didn't want to say that all Extras are thieves but unfortunately it had to be one of us that let everyone down! Anyhow I guess we were being told so we didn't get the same idea.

The 3rd AD placed me on the main table that was being filmed between Matt de Angelo and Kelly Adams and we were supposed to had been playing all night and this was now six in the morning. The good thing was that I felt so sick that I pulled off the six 'clock in the morning look quite well.

Either I was never filmed or I did okay as the 1st AD never actually spoke to me once, not even to ask my name!

At one point during the day there was a noise that was really loud during takes.

At first no one could figure out where this noise was coming from. The boom operator was getting more and more annoyed until finally he could take no more of it and shouted "Stop shuffling those bloody papers!" just before we turned over.

It was only when we cut that Matt said "That was Vaughny with the paper noise. Somebodies only gone and given him some sweets to play with."

I looked over at the next table and sure enough there's the one and only Robert Vaughn sitting down comfortably, taking no notice of anybody else and sticking a boiled sweet into his mouth with a stack of sweet wrappers in front of him!

The morning seemed to go on forever with the scene being shot from every angle imaginable with every lens in the box. Or maybe it simply was because I wasn't well.

My partner was placed on the table with Robert Vaughn.

We stopped for lunch and some people were told to change to be different people but those of us who had been seen would not need to change.

We figured we'd be wrapped and I could go home to bed. Alas no. After lunch there was a change of plan and all of us seen were also to get changed and wait in the bus until needed.

Three minute to five and the 2nd AD came in to say that we were wrapped and would not be needed. That was 3 minutes to overtime! Typical. But I was so glad to get home.

<u>Five Days – Actor's Double / Train Passenger / Railway Employee</u>

Thursday 17th September 2009

This was filmed on a train up in Derbyshire. It was toward the end of the shoot and as far as I knew, I was going to play a train passenger.

We had breakfast at the station and then boarded the train. I sat in my seat reading a book looking forward to simply being able to sit there all day reading and getting paid for it. (Is that lazy or simply being a keen reader?)

Then costume came along and told me that I was going to be playing a railway employee and later on would have to get out onto the tracks, as someone was supposed to have jumped off a bridge and been run over. I wondered who that would be.

I got dressed in my orange florescent jacket and hard hat and sat in my train seat until I was called for.

I was in a seat towards the front of the train with only a couple of Extras. The others had gone to the back of the train away from the crew. I mention this as I think they had mistaken me for someone else, who must have been elsewhere on the train. Anyway, while I was sitting there, a man came along and told me that I was a double for one of the actors.

I said I hadn't been made aware of this but did as I was asked and followed him to the costume team again.

They said I would be playing the train employee later but for now I was to double for the actor who throws himself off the bridge.

Normally I wouldn't think much of this but on this occasion the actor in question was an Asian man dressed as an Asian woman, complete with burka!

It took a surprisingly long time for the burka to be wrapped around my head.

The train had stopped and a makeshift gangplank had been made for us to get off and climb the bank to the bridge where my costume was finalised. I was then placed onto a box to look over the parapet.

The shot was from the train looking up at me, and from the side of the bridge. (You can actually tell it's me even under all that costume by the way I slouch when I walk! And I know this because my wife pointed me out as soon as she saw the trailer for the show)

I didn't have to throw myself off the bridge or even lie on the tracks but I was quickly changed, without ever managing to get a photograph of the outfit, back into my railway employee costume, in which I appeared in the next scene, waving the train on after the accident. Finally I was changed back into my own clothes and became a passenger on the train that I had just stopped by jumping off the bridge and started off again by waving it on! Talk about a busy day. No time for reading.

I got a call to ask if I wanted to go back onto Waterloo Road the next day, as the teacher again, but I turned it down and in fact decided to leave that particular agency as that was all they seemed to offer me nowadays.

<u>Marple – Villager</u>

Monday 18th/Tuesday 19th/Saturday 23rd /Sunday 24th January 2010

The first couple of days were spent on location outside in a village covered in snow. I was so lucky as my character got to ride a bicycle. This was great on 2 accounts.

1- I didn't get my feet cold in the snow

2- I got extra money for riding it. The weird thing is with riding a bike is that you get the same money as driving a car!

Another lucky thing is that as it's a period show, the clothes are really thick and warm in the chilly cold weather.

This was my first time seeing Julia Mckenzie play Miss Marple. She was very funny and sweet and not at all what I expected.

After a few days outside the location changed to a courthouse so as per usual we went to Kingston upon Thames to the courthouse.

I like being out of shot on the Agatha Christie shows as they keep getting me back as I'm not seen but on this occasion whilst sitting well away from the camera I couldn't actually fit in the seat because my legs were too long. I made the mistake of mentioning this to the 3rd AD and I was moved. Unfortunately I was moved directly behind Kevin McNally so I couldn't not be in shot.

It was a pleasure watching the filming of this episode as there were some brilliant actors in this episode , Toby Stephens and Claudie Blakey (Both from Severence) Joanna Page , Claire Rushbrook and Sir Donald Sinden to name just a few.

I usually get bored in court scenes but I did enjoy the days on this and it would end up being my final 'Marple' as the 2nd AD came up to me on the final day and said he was sorry, he knows how much I enjoy the Agatha Christie shows but because I was so in shot I'd not be allowed back for the rest of the season.

I had a great chat with Kevin McNally and I mentioned I had heard that they were going to film the 4th Pirates of the Caribbean film in the UK.

He laughed at me and said "The UK?" "Why would they film it here?"

I felt very silly.

They did in fact shoot the 4th one in the UK. I guess he just wasn't allowed to tell me.

<u>The Jury</u>

Series 2 - Sunday 13th March 2011

It was the first day of production or the second series of "The Jury" (To be honest I hadn't heard of a first season) and I'd got myself a nice featured role on the show as a guy called "Thomas Dent"

The costume had phoned me previous and asked me to bring quite a lot of clothes as I'm suited today and more casual in the following days (which are way ahead at the end of May)

I got to the base in South London and told the security chap on the gate that I'm an Extra for the show and he told me all the Extras need to park their cars over the other side of the road. Typical!

I parked up and wish costume had not asked me to bring quite so much due to having to lug it all the way back to base.

I'd arrived at 06.30 which was an hour early and to wait until my call time to see costume and make-up but I had dropped my partner off at her location for the day on another set.

The runner had given me some sides to read to understand what I was doing today. It seemed simple enough, just walk into a house with an actress and I'm to keep my face away from the camera.

It seemed a lot of trouble to get me there but to not show who I was but I'm sure there's a plan.

I went into Make-up department and they mentioned to me that I'm actually the murderer in this show all along and the 2nd AD told me I'll get hanged later on!

It still didn't make much sense to me and no one mentioned any of this to me when I got the role but alas no matter how featured you are, at the end of the day they only ever tell us what we need to know and to do as we're told.

One of the Background working today was a good friend of mine called Vincent. He's another big Doctor who fan so today simply became talk Science fiction crap all day! I loved it.

I sat there waiting all day but finally made it on set at 17.30 and was finished by 18.00.

I was sent back to base to sign out as quick as possible (to cut down on Overtime payments) and so I shared the car with the actress (Elizabeth Conboy) and she was very polite to me considering she knew what I was.

We chatted on the way back to base about the cancellation of future

Marple or Poirot films (As they've come to an end) and how this was a great shame and also with this being the last season of "Spooks"

So when Elizabeth said to me (politely as she was ever so nice) "You should write your ideas down and send them to the BBC as a letter" I realised I'd just made a seriously big mistake and now she was quite blatantly thinking "What a stupid Extra" but was simply too polite to say it.

At that point I noticed my mistake and shut up the rest of the way to base. I'm not back until May so with luck she'll forget me by then!

The Jury

Thomas Dent - Thursday 5th May

Back in Kingston upon Thames again but today I wasn't being shot in the courthouse room.

I'd gotten to set just in time to get breakfast as they were about to pack up. The stunt team introduced themselves to me having phoned a couple of days ago to check that I would be okay doing my own stunt.

The problem was that fact they'll need to see my face so being doubled would be too difficult.

I grabbed some breakfast and went into the dining room where the actors and the Extras were all sitting and suddenly people were talking to me by my character name.

When I say people I mean the likes of Julie Walters, the main artistes plus the Extras. I was baffled as to how everyone knew me.

The thing was, they had spent weeks on set with the court case and knew what I had done before I did and there were some photos of me in the court that had been sitting in front of everyone for ages (It turned out that my character had found some girls via the internet and killed 3 of them before killing himself and I only learnt this via the court actors today)

I ate up and was sent straight to set to do a rehearsal.

Set for me today was upstairs in one of the office rooms that had been dressed as my bedroom

The stunt team were brilliant. I was going to be hanged! It was a big harness that you sit in like a nappy but it also has leg stirrup as that is where the pressure goes when you're hanging.

I was strung up and had to keep my legs very straight. It's not easy with your own body weight pushing against your feet plus having to play dead.

The director came in and said how he would like my head laying. It was important as the blood had to have rushed to one side of my head as I'd been dead for 2 days and was on the verge of smelling bad.

The stunt team wanted me to have wet marks between my legs as if I had wet myself but the costume department decided against it. I didn't mind either way.

After the rehearsal was sent down to make-up and costume.

Costume gave me my own changing room. I felt special as they provided the costume as well. Granted it was an awful costume and the sparks kept making fun of my jumper!

From there I went to make-up and had my hands made up to a very dark blue colour to represent the cold blood.

Before they could start on my face I was asked back to set again. I was with the second unit so I didn't really get to speak to the main unit much but the second unit were brilliant as they had time to do what they wanted as sets are usually racing against the clock.

Back on set I undressed and the harness was put on. The costume department had thoughtfully got me some cycling shorts to help alleviate the pressure.

Once the stunt guy had strapped me in and tightened it all up, I dressed over the harness. On set there is no time to get shy with a whole bunch of crew standing around whilst I dressed.

I was again hooked up and the crew all watched to decide where to place the camera.

Although I had been hanging for 2 days, they still thought it nice if I swung around a little.

It took so long to strap me in that I said I didn't mind being left in the harness as I was sent back to make-up for my face.

It took 2 hours to make me up dead. The other Extras said I looked like I had been down a coal mine but I suggested they keep those opinions to themselves as make-up would not be best pleased.

I had lunch after make-up and then was sent to set. It got so hot hanging up there that I started to sweat. Not good but some ice packs and a fan were brought in to cool me down. The stunt guys took the piss and said I was acting like a movie star now with the fans an all.

They did a wide, some shots of my face, my hands and then onto my feet.

I suggested I take the stirrups off for the feet shot.

The stunt team said this wasn't a good idea as the feet are keeping me safe from the rope around my neck.

I made a promise that if for one moment, I felt the noose around my neck, I would speak up.

So against the wishes of the stunt team I let them take my stirrups off to get a shot of my feet

Now I understood at this point why they were there in the first place as the fake wire noose was starting to pressurise my neck.

At first it was alright but it was tough trying to stay as still as possible so that I would just swing gently around but as the moments went on, I could feel the world around me fading and I was blacking out.

They had told me to say if I was uncomfortable I tried to hold off for one last take but I'm sure it was taking forever and I got to a point when I could no longer hear them. It was like they were fading of into the background and all I could here was my own head explaining to me that I'm going to die shortly.

With the moments of consciousness I had left as I simply was blacking out so I called the Stunt co-ordinators name.

Quickly they grabbed a box for me to stand on whilst he cut the rope off.

He was a tad angry that I'd not said I was in trouble but I didn't like to say anything as they were still filming.

Once we finished there, I was sent back with costume and make-up to get cleaned up and changed for another shot of me working on the computer in my house. (although a room in the court house doubled for both my kitchen and my bedroom)

The make -up was a blighter to get off. It was stuffed so far down my ears!

I changed and was sent straight back upstairs for the next shot.

They had a very clever thing set up with the computer as it didn't matter what keypad I press, the correct letters come up on screen.

I've watched so many shows where the actors are not pressing the correct letters on the keypad but their typing is perfect and now I knew why so I decided to learn the script and press the correct letters.

In the scene I was on a chat-up site talking to one of the girls that I would end up killing.

I had such a great time with my own little crew. I wanted to get a photo with the clapper board but they had a single shot of the screen to do without me and I was being ushered down the stairs to wrap so I said goodbye and am in fact looking forward to watching this to see what naughtiness my character got up to!

The Jury Thomas Dent

Friday 27th May 2011

I was supposed to be in yesterday but I got cancelled. The thing was I had turned down 2 other jobs before I got cancelled. Unfortunately that's the nature of this business!

Both my partner and I were booked for 09.00 but I got a call at 22.00 the night before to say not to bother coming in before 17.00.

We took separate cars and I arrived at 14.00 only to find that there was no space left on the location lot to park so I had to pay for parking and claim the money back.

Within the hour of me turning up, my partner was wrapped but her car was trapped in the lot, so we swapped cars and she went home!

I was left with 2 other people I know, one was actor turned Extra Adam (If I make a film, he's starring in it!) and his partner Lauren . They were booked to play Doggers in a car. I found this jolly amusing and awaited my fate.

Considering how featured or at least how important my role has been on the series, I was never told anything about who I was playing or what I had to do.

It turned out to be the final day shooting on this show and it felt like the crew just wanted the day to finish.

I waited patiently. I had brought my own lunch as we were told we'd get a meal allowance for the day but not fed!

Later in the day I was asked to go to costume and make-up. It was there that I found out that I was supposed to be watching the doggers whilst sniffing drugs! Well I hadn't expected that one!

They dressed me in Thomas Dents out of date fashion creepy jumper and trousers and greased my hair a little!

Much later on we were able to move the cars as they were filming our scene in the base car park. I moved the car out onto the road and came back to find out what I was going to do.

The cars were placed for the scene. Lauren and Adam got in the back seat and I was given a van. On my way to the van the 3rd AD said Hello and said "John, I'm sorry but have they told you what you've got to do?"

With that comment, I knew straight away what I was expected to be doing. I said "Am I wanking yes?"

She nodded and with that we went off to see the director and a props chap.

Now, I've lived a very boring life and was completely unaware of what poppers were or how they affect you so the prop guy explained to me about poppers and how they affect you when you sniff them (It was actually a pot of scented water)

So I got into my van seat and all the crew just stood around the car watching me! They just wanted to go home.

The 1st AD shouted that they were all to go around the corner as I had an embarrassing scene to do and suddenly this became a closed set.

Up to that point I hadn't been embarrassed as I was just playing a part. That's not me sitting in a van watching people have sex and sniffing drugs whilst playing with myself, it's just a character on TV.

The whole thing was a bit weird, I had look like I was playing with myself whilst the camera pointed to my crotch and as it pulls to my face I was to sniff the poppers and orgasm.

The scene must have been okay as we got through it quite quickly but on the other hand, they really wanted to wrap.

Scene complete, we were wrapped and I changed (But alas left my favourite T-shirt on the costume lorry – boo to wrap day!)

I went to sign out and the runner had to sign me as no chit had been pre prepared and the third AD was busy.

It wasn't until I went home that I realised he's missed my travel expenses, my lunch money and I had forgotten to claim for my parking payment - Blighters!

Well at least I had got to play a killer in a TV show. That's kind of nice.

But it was really weird after it aired to have my Mum and Dad tell me they'd watched it and how proud they were of me and that they told their neighbours it was me. What? Embarrassed much?

Appropriate Adult

Friday 18th March 2011

It was days like this that remind me why I do this job as this was one of the best days out for a long time. It's the other Extras that can make or break the day.

I was booked up in Manchester as a Policeman on this show about Fred and Rose West but it was an early start and I was in London until late last night so I didn't start the day in a great mood.

When I got there another Extra had told me that this show particularity likes boiler suits but I was lucky and got a police outfit.

I got dressed and went for breakfast. After breakfast we had to do a costume check line up and it was decided to hold 2 of us back to change us ...you guessed it...into boiler suits!

We got to set which was supposed to be Fred West's garden in Gloucester but was after the first digging had already been started by the police so there were a few deep holes in the mud. It was all jolly exciting

The first scene for us was that we had to put our yellow jackets on, 2 workers had to move a plank, the digger is started and we should put the police tent together.

That's quite a lot of action to give the Extras. We were shown the tent and even the prop guy said it was a difficult tent to put up.

We had a practice with the tent and it took about fifteen minutes to get up which might be a tad long for the scene and it was finally decided to leave it set up and just put it into place over the hole on action.

We did our first take with the camera placed on the roof of the house and a microphone placed in the garden because there was no room for crew in the garden. We were asked not to mime but to speak as we worked.

Well, That morning someone had pointed out a chap that they didn't get on with at their real job called Gary. We decided to adopt this name and call each other Gary though out the scene.

"To me Gary, pass the spade Gary, Thanks Gary, Need help there Gary?" and so on. We managed to keep straight faces throughout.

After the take, the 3rd AD asked us to do it again but the sound man had requested that we are not all called Gary as it sounds silly.

As requested we updated our names as to not upset the sound guy and so we adopted new names "Harry,Larry,Barry and Gary"

Dominic West was playing Fred and although we're generally asked not to speak to the actors, I said Hello at lunch and pointed out that we'd had a great time whacking him on that shoot a few weeks ago.!!!(The Hour)

The afternoon was just as fun when the 3rd AD asked which one of us was going to be in the hole for the next scene. It was an unanimous vote and I was in the hole within moments. The hole now had a good foot of mud in it and it was one of those times that I was glad we're not wearing our own clothes.

During the following scene Dominic West has to look into the hole where I'm standing facing him with a serious face but I was at the edge of frame in the wide lens. He then decided it would be funny to make suggestive faces at me to see if I could keep that straight face during the take.

Being in the hole didn't seem quite as fun after a few hours of standing in the mud and for a final shot of the day the director had asked if they could have a close up of me in my hole from over the shoulder of Dom West but there wasn't enough light left and it was decided to do the shot as a pick up next Tuesday. (This shot was to be played on the television in the show as if it's a newscast)

We wrapped and the Extras got on the bus along with the crew and the actors as the cars weren't ready yet and I ended up sitting next to Dom West and we had a quick chat about some of his other work while the bus drove.

The next moment I thought we had been brought back to base and was a little confused as we'd been brought back to location. The costume department had decided to go back to base too so the Extras were asked to leave the bus and wait. To be fair the actors were calling out that we could all squeeze in together but alas it wasn't to be and we had to wait on location until the bus came back.

Back at base whilst signing out the production runner asked me if I could come back on Tuesday (I'm already back on Monday but at a different location) so they could get that shot of me in the hole. I pointed out that I was booked on another production next Tuesday and she tried everything to get me to cancel it but the one thing I will never do is drop a previous booking and no matter the situation or money as it's best not to do this or you'll get a reputation at the agencies and the work will stop coming in.

I spoke to the first AD and pointed out I'm pre booked and he was fine about it so someone else will come in and have a nice short day with a nice close up next week but it'll still be me in the wide but again no extra is every irreplaceable the audience don't notice us and we can be swapped with similar looking people without people noticing most of the time.

Appropriate Adult – Police Officer

Monday 21st March 2011

I had been looking forward to coming back onto this show. The morning started with all the usual "Good Morning Gary's" and just when you'd think the joke would have worn thin, all the new Extras started on it and now we had about 20 Police men all called Gary.

I was back in the Police uniform today and the shoes were SO tight. We went to location in a field that the crew had dug a seriously massive brilliant hole in. I was a touch jealous that I didn't get to play in that hole as it was so deep and had been dug with a digger but I did get to follow Fred West around the field in. It doesn't sound like much but it doesn't take much to get me excited.

All the other police were placed (Some poor blighter's were right up in the next field) and I was just standing there when the 3rd (Who finally took the time to learn our names) said that I was to keep my distance but follow Fred and his pose around the field.

We did this all day and my feet were ready to fall off but it was nice to know that all the coppers were having the same feet pain.(Is that okay to find it okay when everyone has painful feet?)

The final shot of the day was the press trying to get a shot of Fred west in the van on the way to the field (Typical for TV to shoot scenes out of order) and there were just 2 of us holding back 30 or so press. They were rather naughty. I think people forget you're not a real policeman when you dress up and they find It fun picking on the coppers as it's one of those things you don't get away with in real life...

To be fair I'm sure I have had my fair share of having fun with Extras dressed as Policemen.

I did ask them nicely if they would at least pretend that I was tough and they couldn't get through my barrier but alas no-one took me seriously.

It turns out, the missing shot from Friday (My close-up in the hole that was going to go to someone else) has been moved to Friday so I'm booked to come back on and get back in my hole.

It was also nice hearing all the other Extras talk about Dominic West and how down to earth and friendly he is.

<u>Appropriate Adult</u>
Friday 25th March 2011

I got to base stupidly early to get some parking as we were told the Extras had limited parking. That's what the message said, it said" there is limited parking at base for the Extras so get there early to get close to the base!"

I got there stupidly early but security still put me in the Extras parking area down the road.

It turned out that there were only 3 of us today as well but when I got into costume, the costume girl asked what size shoe I was, I told her I am size 9 and she pointed out that I had been given the size 6 shoes because there wasn't enough in my size. This is why my feet hurt so bad the last time I was on this show but as there were only 3 of us, they let me borrow some shoes from another policeman's outfit that fit.

The first scene was in the police station and as there were only 3 people we had to wipe (Go close to the camera and walk side to side) several times per take to make it look like there were a few of us.

 The other 2 chaps were then wrapped and I was sent to the Extras green room.

 It was an Extras heaven. I had 2 big boxes of 100 assorted biscuits just sitting there waiting to be eaten!

I was then changed before lunch into costume number 2 for the day and that was a police boiler suit again (I've already mentioned just how much this show likes it's boiler suits)

Just as I was being sent to the mini bus or the next location which was 25 miles away, the costume department said I need to change my shirt (Which was quite well hidden under the boiler suit) and so I missed the mini bus.

I was asked to drive to the next location which was back at Fred West's house (Only this house is based in North Manchester and we were South Manchester).

The next scene was brilliant as I followed the actors down the stairs into the basement and when Robert Glenister shouts at me to tear the wall down so I don my goggles and ear protectors and start bashing the fake wall down with a big sledge hammer.

It wasn't just Dominic West doing the south west accent today as all the crew have now started doing it.

Break time and there were more cakes than any extra could dream of. I was so greedy and ate four!(Maybe I shouldn't have told you that) Well I didn't want to ruin the reputations of Extras..

Finally, I was sent upstairs to change in the "Hole Suit" which is pretty much the boiler suit with some yellow Fisherman waterproofs on top.

I got back into the hole for the final shot of the day and got to give Fred West a nice dirty look and this time Dom West didn't try and make me laugh.

Appropriate Adult

Tuesday 29th March 2011

I arrived at 05.45 for a 07.30 call time. I can never seem to judge the roads correctly but I was a good trained Extra and parked at the back of the building as requested the last time by the gate security man. I walk around the building and checked with him if that's where the Extras park.

I got onto the bus and waited. The 3rd AD finally came to see me and let me read the call sheet. It's a 2 scene day but one of those scenes is nearly seven pages long and it all takes place in a small room at the end of the corridor so myself and another Extra would be wiping in deep background.

It turned out that the other extra was the man who shared my uniform! It works like this. There are 10 police uniforms on hire and there are 2 people named on each uniform so if one is unavailable then the other one can replace.

You'd think with 10 uniforms, 20 names and only 2 Extras booked today the odds of being for the same uniform are slim. Well slim or not, we were both down for the same one. I ended up in somebody else's outfit as I don't have tiny pixie sized feet. It was a nice shoe size but the outfit was a tad big.

Not to worry, just a lot of background wipes today. It was jolly nice day though as I know most of the crew now and Dom West and Now even Emily Watson have got used to seeing me around and doesn't ignore me. I think it's easier for people to bring themselves to talk to us when there's only a few of us.

It helps when the extras are well behaved, don't talk too much and never ask for autographs. Asking for autographs on set is a sackable offence!

Anyhow I asked Emily to sign 3 DVD covers for me today. Red Dragon, Gosford Park and Equilibrium. She was cool and promised to keep hush. If my agents are reading this then I won't be working much longer, but hey, she was sitting by me and I happened to have them in my bag..... in a cardboard protective cover.......in a large envelope.......with a good Sharpie pen.!, Hey , Who doesn't have these things at hand just in-case an Oscar nominee sits by you !

I think this has to be my last time on the show.

Midsomer Murders - SOCO
Monday 18th April 2011

We got to base which was a private estate near High Wycombe. It had been a while since we'd seen a lot of the crew so we said our Hellos and got into costume and then were driven to set.

On the way we saw a set of stones very much like Stonehenge which looked so real but ended up being the set and they were made out of fibre glass. Brilliant.

One of the extras on this show is a guy called Bob who takes being an Extra very seriously and watches every show he does and talks about actors like they're demi-gods. He's been doing Midsomer Murders for quite a few years and I'm sure he believes it's all real.

Today he was going mad with his camera. It's a big fat rule that we don't ever take photos on set but Bob couldn't stop himself today and got very carried away taking photos of extras, crew and the sets.(He's a lovely chap is Bob)

I got given a prop camera to take photos of the dead body and for the first time on set, it was a real working camera with a memory card.

We spent the whole day in a field and there were no toilets so everyone had to go in the hedge if they wanted to go. I thought I could hold out until lunch time but they even brought lunch to set and I didn't want to wee in the bushes so I got a lift back to base with the girls.

Filming in a field all day is not as fun as it sounds

<u>Midsomer Murders -SOCO</u>
Wednesday 22nd June 2011

We got to set 3 hours early and waited in the bus until we were signed in. There a few of us SOCOs and a couple of police.

This was a very fast day with just one shot within one scene. It was a brutal scene though as we were looking into the evidence surrounding the death of a Nun in a chicken pen along with a bunch of dead chickens.

They were real chickens simply torn apart in the pen with heads and wings all over the place. I'm not sure how the show will explain that no animals were harmed in the making of it as these were very real and very dead. They were covered in flies and were starting to smell!

One scene and wrapped plus during this day my diary had started to fill up for the next couple of weeks and I'm going back to Jack the giant killer!

<u>Midsomer Murders – SOCO</u>
Tuesday 23rd August 2011

I've done Midsomer Murders many many times as the same thing (A SOCO and I'm so sorry I've lost so many of my notes for these filming days) but I still can't believe that this particular costume woman still doesn't know who I am (I know, all Extras look the same) and still asks if I've ever been in before!

The scary thing with this job was that whilst we were waiting in the bus, the 2nd AD came in checked who was here. He pointed out that 2 of us weren't actually booked! Our agent had made a mistake. He could easily have sent us home but he very kindly didn't so there were 8 SOCOs today instead of 6.

Today's murder was that of a poor chap who was found in the mud. It wasn't warm outside the mud so I didn't envy the actor who'd died.

Our usual 3rd AD was ill today so a replacement was brought in and I guess some shows are quite difficult to AD if you don't know the procedures (I know new 3rds have big trouble on Holby) of the people that the Extras are playing. It's easy for us as we do the same thing every time we're in but she did well. I do feel for people on dailies for shows especially in the AD department as I can see its quite hard coming into an established show where you're the last to know how things usually work

Midsomer is one of the worst paying jobs but it's such a nice production to work on that no one really cares about the money.

We finished late again and I had to get back to Birmingham as my partner had done this job with me.

Midsomer Murders - SOCO
Tuesday 25th October 2011

We had all been booked on this job weeks prior to doing it but it was only late the night before that we found out that it was a night shoot. This was a shame as I had to turn down 2 days' work Wednesday and Thursday just in case I couldn't get to Cardiff in time from London.

The call time was 20.45 and I got there just as they started lunch.

After lunch I was asked to go to costume and a little disappointed that the costume woman still asks if I've ever been on the show before! She's been asking me this for the last 2 years!

There were 4 SOCOs tonight and we weren't needed for a while so we were asked to wait on the bus until just gone midnight.

Finally just when I was ready to fall asleep on the bus we were taken to set. I was pleased to see James Callis on set.

Now I had met James Callis several times before and it had become a bit of a joke with my friends that I was his accidental stalker!!

I had bumped into him in the street in Liverpool after seeing a play once and then a few weeks later he had walked past me in Trafalgar square and then again down a random street in London with his family but I'd not seen him since Battlestar Galactica had finished on Television so it was nice to get a chance to say that I had enjoyed the ending.

The scene was simply taking photos of a gargoyle that had been used to kill somebody and we weren't on set for more than 30 minutes.

<u>Midsomer Murders - SOCO</u>
Monday 14th November 2011

It was nice to go back to MM. On this show everyone is nice. I had to park in a field at some farmhouse in Slough.

It was a day when we would be needed for nearly every scene. There were only 2 SOCOs though for scenes that needed a few.

We ended up walking backwards and forwards most of the day.

The sound guy had bought himself a new white van. This had been modified to become the new SOCO van!

It was jolly cold though and I'm still not sure as to why the SOCOs have to wear this specific Forensics T-shirt under our outfits because no one can see them and it means we can't put any layers on.

It's at times like these you want to be dressed as a nice wrapped up policeman!

At the top of one scene I start by talking to Neil Dudgeon who plays DC Barnaby but to be fair, even though he's always so nice and friendly I just couldn't think of anything to say to him. I don't watch Midsomer Murders and I'm not a fan of detective shows. (Outside of Peter Gunn but I'm not sure they'll be making any more of them anytime soon.)

We had to wait outside between shots and it was jolly cold but the Background bus was simply too far to put us as we needed to be close to set.

<u>Midsomer Murders (Death of a Diva) – SOCO</u>

Wednesday 25th April 2012

Midsomer is always a nice job as the crew and the cast are lovely but this was just a fleeting visit. We were called at lunch time so we had our lunch and sat in the bus most of the afternoon until a runner was sent to pick us up.

The scene was in a nice house with Egyptian writings all over the walls. It was a very fast scene and I literally walk out from a corner toward the dead body and bend down at my SOCO box.

We did this a few times and we were wrapped. Nice. I do like short days.

<u>Midsomer Murders (Death of a Diva) – SOCO</u>

Monday 30th April/1st May 2012

I got booked back on Midsomer for a couple of days and this time we were sent to a lovely village near Maidenhead.

On the first day we could see a sign up on the local pub advertising a "Stella Harris Film Festival" and we were making little jokes to each other that we should go but then when we went on set for the first time it turned out that Stella Harris was a character from the show.

They had mixed Hammer Horror photos and books with fake Stella Harris merchandise to make it look as if she was a character from the 60s

There was some cool DVDs in the room too plus the art department had made some fake covers for the Stella Harris films.

There were 4 SOCOs and 4 police and we all got a few days out of it and it was the usual dead body stuff and as usual we don't get seen as we have the full face mask and the like on but on the last day we were asked to change into casual clothes. I asked why. They said it was because we were going to become Midsomer locals!

I was so excited. I've never been a local in Midsomer before. Having spent the last few years behind a Mask in the show I was finally going to be me.

The funny thing was that we were placed outside another house in the village square watching the police go back and forward and the next day we were the SOCOs walking in and out of the house.

The days were long though and this was going to be a very tiring week but you can never get enough of working on this show.

<u>Midsomer Murders - SOCO</u>
Sunday 6th May 2012

Just another SOCO day

Midsomer Murders (Written in the stars) – SOCO

Friday 25th May 2012

It was a new story on Midsomer Murders but we weren't there long. The scene was quite long but it was the first scene of the day and it was filmed in a place called "Christmas Common" How cool is that name?

I didn't even see much of what was going on but we got a scorpion on set as it was supposed to have been found in the car.

My job was to simply dust the car for prints. I did this for a few hours and to be fair it's jolly hot in those outfits and masks as the sun was very bright but I want to be a Doctor who monster so I promised myself I would deal with it.

The production had built a fake observatory on the hill. It was brilliant. The final shot of the scene was me dusting the car window for prints. So typical I get a full on face close-up and yet there I am wearing a face mask and a blue hood!

Midsomer Murders

Written in the Stars – SOCO
Friday 1st June 2012

This is the first Friday of the month and that means it's my night out at Doctor Who night in Derby with my friends. I was pleased to see that we were only required for the first scene of the day on this show. Unlike Wizards Vs Aliens, these people trust us enough to give us sides and call-sheets.

The scene was nice and easy. Poor Kenny had been killed in his garden and we were looking around in our blue smurf outfits for the clues as per usual.

There was absolutely NO mobile phone signal in this village at all! I got several text messages through but was unable to telephone anyone. I had a missed call from my main agent and missed that job plus I had a text from Invisible woman people to say I'm now only needed for one day! BOO!

Half way through the scene whilst they turned around, Tamzin Malleson spoke to us and asked if we would dance for her video she's making for her other half who's made an Olympics song. It was only the other day that we found out that her partner was Keith Allen so we thought this would be fun.

It seems they're going to upload the video on the internet and tell the public to make their own!

We did a silly dance and it was fun plus we had a photo with her in return .

We were wrapped quite early so we got our money, got changed and went to the cars, I was looking forward to going to Derby.

Suddenly the 2nd AD appeared at our car window "Do you mind staying until the last scene as you might be seen out of the window"

What could we say? We had to do it. If only we had escaped seconds earlier as he wouldn't have been able to telephone us!

We waited all day just for a stupid shot from inside the house as the actors are talking to each other we're outside. I have no idea if we're seen but we wrapped at 19.30 so no night out.

<u>Midsomer Murders - The Sicilian Defence – SOCO</u>

Wednesday 18th July 2012

Today we were in Rickmansworth. Hmmm, we used to be based much more toward Oxford area but now to seem to be drifting slowly toward London.

It was a nice 12.15 start time but to my surprise it was down to be a Midnight finish as our agent had forgotten to tell us this little piece of information.

When we got there Tamsin asked us if we'd seen ourselves in the new Keith Allen Olympics song video they'd posted. I said we had and thanked her for including us in it.

Today's Midsomer scene was poor Richard Lumsden lying dead on the bridge.

As my partner and I play SOCOs we only ever get to see the dead bodies but alas today it rained. And rained and rained. Our paper SOCO suits were soaked through. In fact everyone on set was soaked through.

One small advantage of being closer to town was the fact that my mobile telephone has a signal (Midsomer always seem to be filming where there is no signal) and thus I got a call to say I'm on Silent witness tomorrow.

<u>Midsomer Murders - SOCO</u>
Monday 20th August 2012

I'd heard this was going to be the final season of Midsomer so I thought this might be my last ever visit as this season finishes next week and I'm not back on it as I am soon to give up the Background work to get a real job and make my own film (You laugh. But I actually did it) It turned out they've been commissioned for another season next year.

The location today was a chalk mine that was doubling as the "Midsomer Cheese Dairies!" and my job was to photograph poor dead Martine McCutcheon. She had been killed by cheese!

Seriously. I love it. Fantastic.

She was very nice and I told her I'd met her on set some years ago. I wasn't sure what commercial it was and she said it was Lenor fabric conditioner.

This was pretty much all I did today but I did have a telephone call from my agent up North. I was booked on a job called "The making of a Lady" and I was to go for my fitting this Thursday but the make-up woman who had phoned me at the weekend had managed to kindly get me cancelled as I said I could not promise to have my hair cut between now and mid-September when I was actually booked for. How could I make such a promise? I'm just an Extra that has a haircut when the productions feel like cutting it and I imagine this would have been a very low paid job anyhow as they were only paying £20 for the entire fitting and that includes travelling all the way up to Manchester with my own fuel costs. Not to worry. Something else would come along.

<u>Midsomer Murders – Policeman /party guest</u>

Tuesday 24th June 2014

I'd never been a Policeman in Midsomer Murders. I'd spent a few years as a SOCO but this was my first time as a Policeman so I was quite pleased. I met up with my friend Andy and he drove us to Gaydon to meet the Police agent who provided me with the costume. It must have looked dodgy getting a Police Uniform out of his boot and putting it in ours!

We then drove down to someplace off the M25 and signed in. It was weird how so many of the crew had changed. I had a brilliant Breakfast as always on this show and then we went to set. We never quite made it onto set but Neil Dudgeon came out and said "Good Morning officers".

That was nice but we never actually got in front of the camera. We were asked to go back to the bus and relax!

Well relax we did. We talked crap all morning as it was just the 2 of us. My wife was on the set of "Silent witness" and we wondered what ever became of Amanda Burton?

I decided I wanted a poo but refused to go all day because I am still traumatised about the Foyles War incident a few weeks back!

I mention this because we were asked to change into suits for another scene at 18.30. This is 11 hours after starting!

We go back onto set and who should walk past us? Amanda Burton. She saw us starring in disbelief and said Hello. Andrew Lee Potts was about too.

The director on this episode was Charlie Palmer. He was the director on a Poirot I was on but was never really in shot some years ago and he was director of that episode By Any Means" where I was the vicar with over 100 words of Dialogue only for the whole thing to be cut and a voice over did my voice on a wide.

I don't for a minute think Charlie Palmer doesn't like me being in front of his camera. Yes, he'd decided not to have me as a policeman in the morning but still I didn't think anything of it until...

The scene was set up and for my part, I get out of a car in my usual TV detective suit and tie. This was chosen by costume as I was told smart.

But then he made a comment to the crew and it seems all the party guests had to be in Black Tie attire!

I was asked to step aside and never got used at all. Does Charlie Palmer hate me that much'? I'm sure I'll see him on set again someday and we'll see if it's all coincidence

Epilogue

There are so many missing stories. I have dates and photos from episodes and shows that I have no idea what happened but these are some of the Crime shows I've had the pleasure of being on.

I hope you enjoyed it and again do look out for "Extra Time" , Stories from a Doctor Who TV Extra plus the forthcoming More Stories from Crime TV Extra, Stories from a Movie Extra, Stories from a TV Soap Extra and others.

I hope to have Extra Time 2 out in 2024

Available now from Amazon in Book form or Kindle

About Extra Time

"It's a Brilliant book, Fascinating"
Caroline Munro

"It's a great read"
Derek Martin

"You must read it"
Martin Stephens (Village of the Damned- 1960)

Printed in Great Britain
by Amazon

27807411R00116